B. J. SURHOFF
CATCHER

MILWAUKEE
BREWERS

GORMAN THOMAS
CENTER FIELDER

MILWAUKEE
BREWERS

THE STORY OF THE MILWAUKEE BREWERS

Published by Creative Education
P.O. Box 227, Mankato, Minnesota 56002
Creative Education is an imprint of The Creative Company
www.thecreativecompany.us

Design and production by Blue Design
Art direction by Rita Marshall
Printed by Corporate Graphics in the United States of America

Photographs by Getty Images (Bernstein Associates, Scott Boehm, Jonathan Daniel, Elsa, Focus on Sport, Otto Greule Jr, Bruce Kluckhohn, Tom G. Lynn/Time & Life Pictures, Brad Mangin/MLB Photos, Jim McIsaac, Ronald C. Modra/Sports Imagery, Panoramic Images, Rich Pilling/MLB Photos, Eliot J. Schechter, Ron Vesely/MLB Photos)

Library of Congress Cataloging-in-Publication Data

Gilbert, Sara.
The story of the Milwaukee Brewers / by Sara Gilbert.
p. cm. — (Baseball: the great American game)
Includes index.
Summary: The history of the Milwaukee Brewers professional baseball team from its inaugural 1970 season to today, spotlighting the team's greatest players and most memorable moments.
ISBN 978-1-60818-046-2
1. Milwaukee Brewers (Baseball team)—History—Juvenile literature. I. Title. II. Series.

GV875.M53G55 2011
796.357'640977595—dc22   2010024403

CPSIA: 110310 PO1381

First Edition
9 8 7 6 5 4 3 2 1

Page 3: First baseman Prince Fielder
Page 4: Right fielder Corey Hart

BASEBALL: THE GREAT AMERICAN GAME

THE STORY OF THE MILWAUKEE BREWERS

Sara Gilbert

FIEDER
28

CREATIVE EDUCATION

CONTENTS

BREWING UP

The first European settlers in the area that now includes the city of Milwaukee, Wisconsin, were French and French Canadian fur traders in the 1830s. By the late 1840s, German immigrants had joined them in the growing city on the shores of Lake Michigan. Soon, so many Germans had moved to Milwaukee that their language was heard on the city's streets more often than English. Their customs, including brewing hearty beers and serving spicy sausages, became common as well.

That heritage was honored in 1970 when local businessman Allan H. "Bud" Selig bought a floundering, one-year-old American League (AL) team called the Seattle Pilots, brought it to Milwaukee, and renamed it the Brewers. Selig had been trying to bring baseball back to his hometown ever since the Milwaukee Braves had moved to Atlanta, Georgia, five years earlier. So even though his purchase of the Pilots became final just six days before the start of the 1970 season, he was determined to put the team on the field for opening day.

Milwaukee has been a hotspot for many diverse activities throughout its history, from fur trading to beer brewing to major-league baseball.

PITCHER · TEDDY HIGUERA

The Brewers discovered Teddy Higuera in the Mexican League. He impressed team scouts enough that they brought him back to Wisconsin, where he surprised everyone by posting 15 wins and finishing second in AL Rookie of the Year voting in 1985. His sophomore season was even better. He won 20 games and finished just behind Boston Red Sox ace Roger Clemens in voting for the Cy Young Award. His reputation as a workhorse (he averaged 237 innings a year from 1985 to 1988) took a hit when he suffered a back injury in 1989. Higuera's productivity waned in the early 1990s, and he was released after the 1994 season.

TEDDY HIGUERA
PITCHER

MILWAUKEE
BREWERS

STATS

Brewers seasons: 1985–94

Height: 5-foot-10

Weight: 178

- **94–64 career record**

- **1,081 career strikeouts**

- **1,380 career innings pitched**

- **1986 All-Star**

There was so little time to prepare for the season that the new Brewers, who included such proven talents as second baseman Tommy Harper and pitcher Lew Krausse, entered County Stadium for the first game wearing the old blue and gold Pilots uniforms with new logos hastily sewn on. The outline of the Pilots logos could still be seen by many of the 37,237 fans who watched the Brewers lose to the California Angels, 12–0.

Although that first season, as well as the next few, ended with losing records, Brewers fans rallied around the team. In 1970, almost one million people crowded into County Stadium to root for the Brewers. "Fans here didn't expect greatness," radio announcer Bob Uecker said. "They respected and cheered the players who worked hard and showed the fans that they were trying. The fans liked that."

In 1972, Milwaukee moved from the AL Western Division to the AL Eastern Division, where it occupied last place in the standings. The team's fortunes didn't seem likely to improve in 1973, either, when a blizzard delayed the home opener by four days. But as the weather improved, so did the team's record. With pitcher Jim Colborn winning 20 games, the Brewers rose out of the division

cellar to finish fifth among the AL East's 6 teams.

Although Milwaukee would not put together a winning season until 1978, when the Brewers finished at 93–69, the team still gave fans reasons to watch in the meantime. Among them was curly-haired shortstop Robin Yount, who joined the team in 1974 at the age of 18, and legendary outfielder Hank Aaron, who returned to Milwaukee in 1975 for the last 2 seasons of his career. (Aaron spent 21 years with the Braves organization, first in Milwaukee and then in Atlanta.) Yount was an exciting young player with a lot of potential, and although the 41-year-old Aaron was past his prime, his presence energized both players and fans. With such headliners in 1975, it was no wonder that a record 1.2 million people visited County Stadium.

Those crowds got to see Aaron hit the final 22 of his 755 career home runs, but they also had to watch the Brewers lose many games. That all changed during the 1978 season. With power-hitting utility man Sal Bando and first baseman Cecil Cooper in the lineup, rookie sensation Paul Molitor at third, and sure-handed Jim Gantner at second, the Brewers suddenly surged to third place in the now seven-team AL East. Their days at the bottom were finally over. "We could all feel it," Yount said later. "We knew we were getting better. We knew that the pieces were fitting into place."

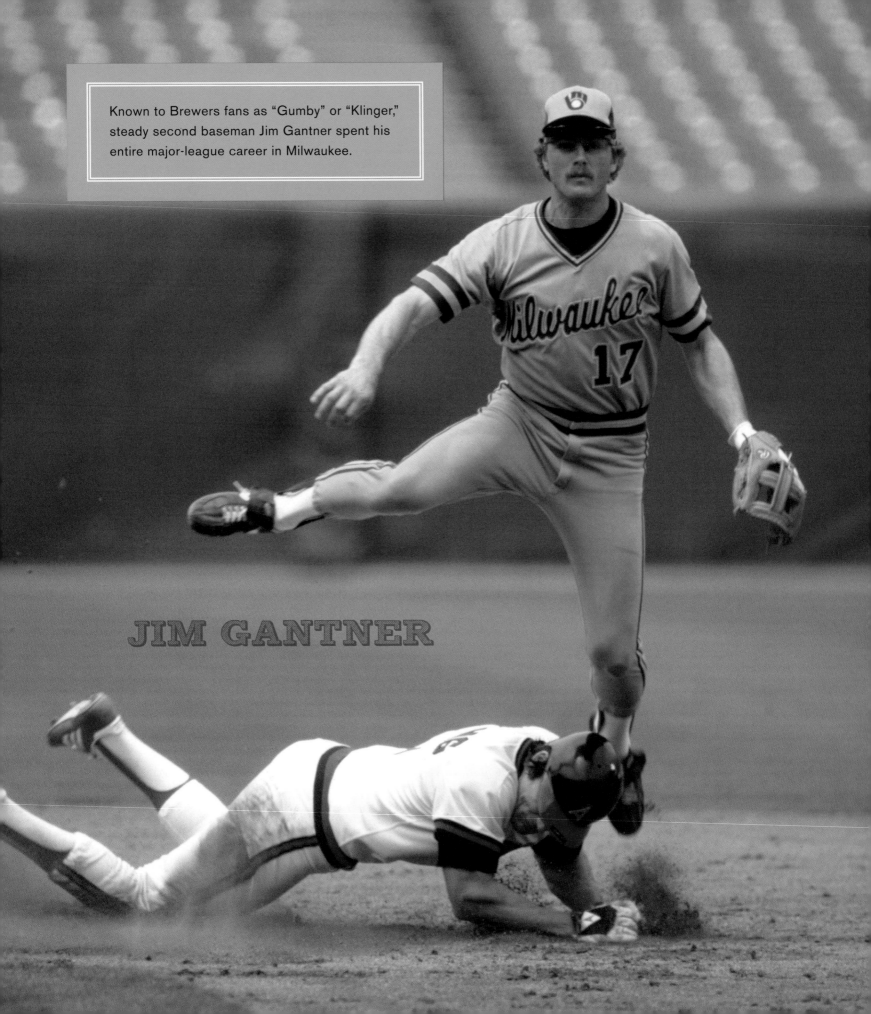

Known to Brewers fans as "Gumby" or "Klinger," steady second baseman Jim Gantner spent his entire major-league career in Milwaukee.

JIM GANTNER

THE MAJOR LEAGUES IN MILWAUKEE

Bud Selig got the call at 10:15 P.M. on March 31, 1970: The bankrupt Seattle Pilots would officially be moving to Wisconsin to begin the baseball season—which was only one week away. But after five years of trying to land a team, Selig wasn't about to complain about the timing. By the time the Pilots arrived in Milwaukee, the city was ready for them. More than 37,000 fans showed up at County Stadium to see the Brewers get flattened by the California Angels, 12–0, in their first game. It took until May 6 for the Brewers to win a game in front of their home fans, a 4–3 victory over the Boston Red Sox. In the midst of an endless string of road trips to the West Coast, part of the Pilots' predetermined schedule, the losses piled up more quickly than the wins. The season even included one tie—a 5–5 stalemate with the New York Yankees, called after a seemingly interminable 10th inning. The Brewers' first season saw them finish with a discouraging 65–97–1 record, in fourth place in the AL West. But Milwaukee fans were just happy to have a team of their own once again.

CATCHER · B. J. SURHOFF

After the Brewers selected him as the first overall pick in baseball's 1985 amateur draft, B. J. Surhoff cruised through the minor-league farm system and joined the big-league team in 1987. He made an immediate impression, hitting .299 and earning a regular spot in Milwaukee's lineup. Although never flashy at the plate or in the field (as a sometime first or third baseman and outfielder), Surhoff was a solid line-drive hitter who rarely struck out or walked. In 1995, he hit a career-high .320. Before the next season, he signed with the Baltimore Orioles, with whom he became a full-time outfielder.

B. J. SURHOFF
CATCHER

MILWAUKEE BREWERS

STATS

Brewers seasons: 1987–95

Height: 6-foot-1

Weight: 185

- **2,326 career hits**

- **1,153 career RBI**

- **.282 career BA**

- **1999 All-Star**

FIRST BASEMAN · CECIL COOPER

Cecil Cooper was an all-around average ballplayer when he arrived in Milwaukee. But once he adjusted his batting stance to mimic that of hot-hitting Minnesota Twins star Rod Carew, he became an offensive powerhouse, slamming 241 home runs and accumulating a .298 batting average during his 17-year career. He hit at or above .300 during his first 7 seasons in Milwaukee, including a .352 season in 1980, but he never won the coveted batting title. Yet "Coop" was always a champ to Brewers fans. His playing days ended in 1987, but Cooper remained in baseball as a coach and became the manager of his home-state Houston Astros in 2007.

CECIL COOPER
FIRST BASEMAN

MILWAUKEE
BREWERS

STATS

Brewers seasons: 1977–87

Height: 6-foot-2

Weight: 165

- **5-time All-Star**

- **2-time Gold Glove winner**

- **2,192 career hits**

- **1,125 career RBI**

WISCONSIN'S WALLBANGERS

ilwaukee started the 1979 season stocked with sluggers, from the clean-cut Cooper to scruffy center fielder Gorman Thomas. The team led the AL with 185 home runs, including 45 from Thomas alone. But despite their power-packed lineup, the Brewers finished the season eight games behind the Baltimore Orioles in the AL East.

On opening day of the 1980 season, right fielder Sixto Lezcano hit a grand slam in Milwaukee's 9–5 win over the Boston Red Sox, kicking off a season-long home run barrage that resulted in the team's compiling a league-leading 203 total home runs. Even though they had one of the most powerful offenses in the majors and assembled an impressive 86–76 record, the Brewers had to settle for third place in the AL East, behind the powerful New York Yankees and Orioles.

Milwaukee management decided to bolster the team by upgrading the pitching staff in 1981. Well-planned trades brought hurler Pete Vuckovich, star closer Rollie Fingers, and veteran catcher Ted Simmons

to Milwaukee. In a 1981 season shortened by a players' strike, Fingers
tallied a league-leading 28 saves on his way to earning both the Cy Young
Award (as the league's best pitcher) and AL Most Valuable Player (MVP)
honors. Vuckovich went 14–4, and Simmons delivered 14 home runs and
61 runs batted in (RBI). Milwaukee finished in first place and earned its
first trip to the playoffs, but it was quickly defeated by the Yankees.

Harvey Kuenn took over as manager in 1982, and the hard-hitting
Brewers quickly became known as "Harvey's Wallbangers." The team
totaled 216 round-trippers and finished the season with a collective
batting average of .279. Yount led the league in seven offensive categories
and had such a spectacular fielding season at shortstop that he was
awarded the Gold Glove award. But it was another honor that Brewers
fans wanted most for Yount: MVP. They made sure he knew they were
rooting for him by chanting "MVP! MVP!" every time he came to the
plate in August and September—and they weren't surprised when he
received the award at season's end.

 After edging out the Orioles to win the division, the Brewers went west
for the first two games of the AL Championship Series (ALCS) against the

ROLLIE FINGERS

SECOND BASEMAN · JIM GANTNER

Jim Gantner was never a spectacular player. The native Wisconsinite was drafted by the Brewers in the 12th round of the 1974 draft and played in Milwaukee for all 17 years of his pro career. During that time, he hit only 47 total home runs and never batted above the .300 mark. But as part of an infield that also included Hall-of-Famers Robin Yount and Paul Molitor, Gantner didn't have to be spectacular. He just had to be dependable—and that he was. Gantner, who was named team MVP in 1984, still ranks among Milwaukee's all-time leaders in games, at bats, and hits.

JIM GANTNER
SECOND BASEMAN

MILWAUKEE
BREWERS

STATS

Brewers seasons: 1976–92

Height: 6 feet

Weight: 180

- **.274 career BA**
- **1,801 career games**
- **1,696 career hits**
- **Brewers' Walk of Fame inductee (2004)**

GORMAN THOMAS

Angels. Although they lost both contests in California, they swept the final three games of the series in Milwaukee. Yount wrapped up the ALCS and sent the team to the World Series by fielding a one-hopper and tossing the ball to Cooper at first. "It seemed like it took five minutes for the ball to get over there," Yount remembered. "I could see it going through the air, and I wasn't sure it was ever going to get to the first baseman."

Harvey's Wallbangers won Game 1 of the World Series against the St. Louis Cardinals 10–0, but the Cardinals took the next two games. After Milwaukee came out on top in Games 4 and 5, St. Louis rolled to a lopsided 13–1 victory in Game 6, then won the deciding seventh game 6–3. Despite the disappointment, more than 100,000 fans welcomed the Brewers back to town with a ticker-tape parade. Yount roared into County Stadium on his motorcycle, pumping his fist in the air and thanking the fans for their loyalty.

That same fan support continued throughout the 1983 season, when a team-record 2,397,131 people jammed into County Stadium to watch

THE VOICE OF THE BREWERS

Bob Uecker will tell you frankly why he's been in the Brewers' broadcast booth for more than 35 years: Because he wasn't good enough to stay on the field that long. But Brewers fans are lucky that the self-effacing Uecker hit only .200 with 14 home runs in his 6-year career. Since becoming the play-by-play announcer for his hometown team in 1971, Uecker's deadpan sense of humor, insider's perspective, and love of the game have made him one of the best baseball broadcasters in the country. His affable personality and comic presence have afforded him opportunities to star elsewhere as well.

He logged more than 100 appearances on *The Tonight Show* with Johnny Carson and has been a guest on the *Merv Griffin Show*, *Late Night with David Letterman*, and *Saturday Night Live*. He also played key roles in the motion pictures *Major League* and *Major League II*. But his biggest honor may have come when he was inducted into the Baseball Hall of Fame as a broadcaster in 2003. True to his nature, Uecker gave one of the most memorable speeches in Hall history, causing most of the audience members (including former president George H. W. Bush) to laugh until they cried.

STREAK CITY

he 1987 season started differently for the Brewers. Molitor was healthy, as was Yount, who had been shifted to center field after suffering a shoulder injury. With those key players in place, the Brewers charged out of the gate, tying a major-league record by winning their first 13 games, including a no-hitter tossed by young southpaw Juan Nieves. By the end of April, they were a remarkable 18–3.

What happened next earned Milwaukee the nickname "Team Streak." On May 3, the Brewers lost 7–3 and proceeded to lose the next 11 games in a row, finally picking up a win over the Chicago White Sox on May 20. Then, when Molitor returned from a hamstring injury in July, he connected for the first hit of what would be the most momentous streak of the season: a 39-game hitting streak that, for a time, seemed as though it would threaten Yankees legend Joe DiMaggio's 56-game record. The streak ended with Molitor waiting in the on-deck circle in the 10th inning of a game against Cleveland. Although the Brewers won the game, fans were devastated that their hero had not had a chance to extend his streak. "People booed," remembered owner Bud Selig.

The Brewers finished in third place that season and fell just two games shy of the division title in 1988. But the momentum stopped there. Despite solid offensive production from Molitor, Yount, and catcher B. J. Surhoff, the team posted disappointing records during each of the next three seasons. At the end of the 1991 season, manager Tom Trebelhorn was replaced by Phil Garner, a former third base coach with the Houston Astros.

Although Garner had three holdovers from the 1982 World Series team—Yount, Molitor, and Gantner—in his 1992 opening day lineup, the rest of the roster was relatively young. But the pitching was surprisingly good, with Chris Bosio and Cal Eldred each putting together 10-game winning streaks and Jaime Navarro winning a team-high 17 games. Garner's aggressive game plan had the Brewers streaking around the base paths, stealing a league-leading 256 bases. Rookie shortstop Pat Listach accounted for 54 of those, setting a club record and winning AL Rookie of the Year honors as the Brewers rallied for a 92–70 finish.

Pat Listach's rookie campaign was by far the best of his career, but still, Brewers fans enjoyed his hustle and hardnosed play for five seasons.

PAT LISTACH

SEASON OF STREAKS

It started simply enough. On April 6, 1987, the Brewers beat the Boston Red Sox 5–1. The next night, they won again. Two weeks later, they were still winning, tying a major-league record with 13 straight victories. But then, on May 3, Milwaukee fell to the Seattle Mariners 7–3. The next night, they lost again. Two weeks after that, there were still losing, tallying 12 straight losses. But "Team Streak" was just getting started. In mid-July, third baseman Paul Molitor launched another streak that lasted an incredible 39 games. During his hitting tear, the longest in baseball since Joe DiMaggio's 56-game spree in 1941, Molitor hit .415 with 68 hits, 7 home runs, and 33 RBI. Then came August 26. Molitor was hitless in the bottom of the 10th against the Cleveland Indians. With outfielder Mike Felder at second, shortstop Dale Sveum at first, outfielder Rick Manning at the plate, and two outs, Molitor stepped into the on-deck circle. The crowd at County Stadium got to their feet as Manning took a called strike. Then, when Manning slapped the next pitch into center field and Felder raced around third to score the game's winning run, they erupted in a chorus of boos despite the win. The last streak of the season was officially over.

PAUL MOLITOR

SHORTSTOP · ROBIN YOUNT

Robin Yount, who joined the Brewers as an 18-year-old in 1974, spent his entire 20-year career in Milwaukee. The dedicated shortstop was an outstanding all-around player known for both his smooth defensive plays (he earned league MVP honors twice while manning the shortstop and center field positions) as well as his strong stroke at the plate. He was also appreciated for his many years of loyalty to the same team, which was impressive, considering that his career began at almost the same time as the introduction of free agency. Yount joined the 3,000-hit club in 1992 and was the first Brewers player elected to the Hall of Fame.

ROBIN YOUNT
SHORTSTOP

MILWAUKEE
BREWERS

STATS

Brewers seasons: 1974–93

Height: 6 feet

Weight: 165

- **3,142 career hits**

- **251 career HR**

- **3-time All-Star**

- **Baseball Hall of Fame inductee (1999)**

While the 1992 season felt like a fresh start to some, for others it marked the end of an era. On September 9, Yount knocked his 3,000th hit with the Brewers. Molitor and Gantner met him at first base to lift him off the ground in a celebratory hug. They had been with him for most of the ride, but that season would prove to be the end of the line for the tight trio. Gantner retired, and Molitor signed with the Toronto Blue Jays. Yount retired a year later, causing emotions to run high in Milwaukee. "I don't think many people understand how rare it is for a player to come to a franchise, play two decades, and never cause one iota of a problem," a choked-up Selig said. "He played the game every single day the way it's supposed to be played."

LEFT FIELDER · BEN OGLIVIE

At a slim 6-foot-2, Ben Oglivie cut a recognizable figure in the field and at the plate. His long arms powered a solid swing that sent many a pitch into the outfield stands. In his second season with the Brewers, the veteran hit 29 home runs and followed that up with a league-leading 41 dingers the next year. His big bat helped lead the team to its first World Series appearance in 1982 and made for several Brewers highlights during the series as well—although his home run in Game 7 wasn't enough to bring a championship to Milwaukee.

BEN OGLIVIE
LEFT FIELDER

MILWAUKEE
BREWERS

STATS

Brewers seasons: 1978–86

Height: 6-foot-2

Weight: 160

- **3-time All-Star**

- **235 career HR**

- **901 career RBI**

- **277 career doubles**

BERNIE BREWER

Home runs at Milwaukee's Miller Park are always celebrated the same way: team mascot Bernie Brewer, with his oversized mustache and festive lederhosen, dances out of his chalet above the bleachers in left field, claps his hands, and jumps down a long yellow chute before bouncing back up and cheering. It's a time-honored tradition that started during the Brewers' first season in Milwaukee—though back then, Bernie was waiting for something else to send him down. The original Bernie Brewer was a fan, 69-year-old retiree Milt Mason, who was disappointed in the paltry turnout at County Stadium. So on July 6, 1970, he ascended to a specially designed trailer at the top of the scoreboard in right field, pledging to stay there until a crowd of at least 40,000 came to the ballpark. He spent 40 days with just a television, an exercise bike, a gas stove, and a telephone before 44,387 fans squeezed into County Stadium to watch the Brewers take on the Cleveland Indians on August 16. In honor of Mason's tenacity, Bernie Brewer officially became the team mascot in 1973. Although stadium renovations forced him into retirement in 1984, fan requests brought Bernie back in 1993.

Miller Park combined classic styling with new technology, featuring an arched, brick-layered exterior and an enormous retractable roof.

CHANGING OF THE GUARD

ithout its longtime leaders, the team floundered, finishing at the bottom of the AL East in 1993 and 1994. When the players returned in 1995 from a strike that cut short the 1994 season, the Brewers started strong and were within a half-game in the AL Wild Card race by the end of August. But the team faded in September and finished in fourth place at 65–79. In 1996, too, the Brewers finished out of playoff contention.

Like the team itself, the Brewers' longtime field, County Stadium, had seen better days. In 1995, the Wisconsin state legislature had passed a financing package allowing for a new ballpark to be built. In November 1996, the Brewers broke ground for Miller Park, and for the next four years, the construction of the state-of-the-art stadium — named for the famous local beer sponsor—was bigger news than the ballclub itself.

Slugging right fielder Jeromy Burnitz helped keep the Brewers afloat during their final years in County Stadium, but the team still finished the 1997 season 78–83 and out of contention. Then Milwaukee jumped from the AL to the National League (NL) as part of Major League Baseball's realignment plan, which placed the Brewers in the NL's Central Division. Although its first month in the older league went well, the team faded fast in 1998 and posted its sixth straight losing season.

Off-the-field news continued to overshadow the team's play in 1999, when Robin Yount became the first Brewers player elected into the Baseball Hall of Fame, and Paul Molitor's number 4 uniform was retired in a ceremony at County Stadium. The biggest news, however, was also the worst: A crane collapsed on the building site of Miller Park, killing four construction workers and delaying the stadium's planned opening by a full year. As the Brewers compiled losing records in their final two seasons in County Stadium, fans hoped that a new ballpark would bring a better future for their hometown team.

Miller Park opened on April 6, 2001, with Selig, who had been serving as the commissioner of baseball since 1992, and president

CENTER FIELDER · GORMAN THOMAS

It's easy to understand why Gorman Thomas became a fan favorite in Milwaukee. The rugged outfielder with the unruly hair would crash into walls to steal home runs from opponents, then send balls over those same walls when it was his turn to bat. Of course, his home run swing missed every now and then: "Stormin' Gorman" struck out a whopping 175 times in 1979—and led the AL with 45 home runs. Milwaukee fans were devastated when the Brewers traded Thomas to the Cleveland Indians in 1983, but they welcomed the slugger home for the second half of his final season in 1986.

GORMAN THOMAS
CENTER FIELDER

MILWAUKEE
BREWERS

STATS

Brewers seasons: 1973–83, 1986

Height: 6-foot-2

Weight: 210

- **1981 All-Star**

- **268 career HR**

- **782 career RBI**

- **2,950 career putouts**

George W. Bush on hand to throw out the ceremonial first pitches. The Brewers won that first game 5–4, courtesy of an eighth-inning home run by slugging first baseman Richie Sexson, and went on to sweep the Cincinnati Reds. "I believe there's a lot of exciting days and nights ahead for many, many years at Miller Park," Brewers manager Davey Lopes said after the series. "I think the anticipation, the excitement, matched everything that everybody expected it to be, and maybe even more."

The excitement built throughout the first half of the 2001 season. Sexson, Burnitz, and outfielder Geoff Jenkins became known as the "Miller Park Mashers" for their powerful bats, and, with their help, the team hit more than 200 long balls during the season. But all of those big swings also helped set a more dubious record—that for most strikeouts in the majors (1,399). Milwaukee fizzled to a fourth-place finish in the NL Central.

After pitcher Ben Sheets earned a win on opening day in 2002, the Brewers lost 12 of their next 15 games for the worst start in team history. Despite the anticipation of hosting that year's All-Star Game at Miller Park, the Brewers couldn't seem to build any

winning momentum throughout the season. Milwaukee settled at the bottom of the division early on and never escaped, assembling a franchise-worst 56–106 record. The dismal season led to a shakeup of the team's front-office staff and to the dismissal of Doug Melvin as the club's manager.

A TALE OF TWO LEAGUES

There was no visible sign of a significant change when the Milwaukee Brewers took the field on opening day of the 1998 season. Most of the same players were wearing the same uniforms and playing in the same stadium as they had the previous year. But something had definitely changed: After 27 years of playing in the American League, the Brewers had switched to the National League. The move had been necessitated by the addition of two expansion teams to the league, which meant that both the NL and the AL had 15 teams total. The odd number of teams created scheduling dilemmas,

and Major League Baseball decided that shifting one team from the AL Central Division to the NL Central Division would solve the problem. Milwaukee owner Bud Selig saw the potential for financial benefit from the move, as the team would be able to build a new rivalry with the nearby Chicago Cubs. Because he was also commissioner of Major League Baseball and wanted to avoid the appearance of having a conflict of interest, Selig gave the option to the Kansas City Royals first. The Royals chose to stay in the AL, and the Brewers then took the opportunity to move.

RIGHT FIELDER · JEROMY BURNITZ

Jeromy Burnitz began his big-league career in 1993 but did not become a power hitter until he joined the Brewers. The outfielder hit 27 long balls in his first full season with the team, 2 of which came in back-to-back pinch-hitting appearances in 1 game. The next season, he slugged a career-high 38 home runs. Burnitz's reputation as a home run hitter was solidified by two memorable accomplishments: He was the team's first representative in baseball's annual Home Run Derby in 1999, finishing second with 14 homers, and he sent the first Brewers ball out of Miller Park when the new stadium opened in 2001.

JEROMY BURNITZ
RIGHT FIELDER

MILWAUKEE
BREWERS

STATS

Brewers seasons: 1996–2001

Height: 6 feet

Weight: 190

- 1999 All-Star

- Career-high 20 stolen bases in 1997

- 315 career HR

- 981 career RBI

MANAGER · HARVEY KUENN

Harvey Kuenn was the Brewers' most memorable manager, despite leading the team for only three seasons. The Wisconsin native, a solid contact hitter during his playing days, first took the helm as an interim manager in 1975 before battling health problems. In 1980, his right leg was amputated just below the knee after a blood clot cut off circulation. He returned to coaching six months later and took control of the team again in 1982—just in time to lead his powerful lineup, known as "Harvey's Wallbangers," to the World Series. Kuenn was fired after the team finished 87–75 in 1983, and he passed away in 1988.

STATS

Brewers seasons as manager:
1975, 1982–83

Managerial record: 160–118

AL pennant: 1982

HARVEY KUENN
MANAGER

MILWAUKEE
BREWERS

A NEW BREW

ew manager Ned Yost, a former Brewers catcher, started the 2003 season hoping for a turnaround. Center fielder Scott Podsednik's phenomenal rookie season—in which he hit .314, stole 43 bases, and scored 100 runs—along with Sexson's second 40-plus homer campaign, helped take some of the sting out of the team's 11th straight losing season. But then Sexson was traded to the Arizona Diamondbacks during the off-season, and Milwaukee fans didn't expect to have much to cheer about in 2004.

The Sexson trade brought in six new players, including first baseman Lyle Overbay, who led the team with a .301 average in 2004, and catcher Chad Moeller, who hit for the cycle in April (getting a single, double, triple, and homer in one game). Thanks to their contributions, the team was above the .500 mark at the midseason All-Star break. But Milwaukee's bats fell silent in the second half of the season, and the team finished in last place again.

The Brewers finished well short of the playoffs again in 2005 and 2006. But there were signs of hope in Milwaukee. For one thing, the power was back on in Miller Park. The team totaled 180 home runs for the season, and in an April 2006 game, 5 players hit home runs in a single inning, tying a major-league record. Among those hitting fence-clearing shots were lumbering first baseman Prince Fielder and spirited young shortstop J. J. Hardy. To help the offense, the team added veteran hurler Jeff Suppan to a talented pitching staff that already featured Sheets and Chris Capuano. "This is a young, dangerous team," said newly signed catcher Johnny Estrada. "It's not just a pushover team."

Milwaukee's performance in 2007 proved Estrada right. Powered by Fielder, Hardy, and the unexpected slugging power of rookie outfielder Ryan Braun, the Brewers finished with a winning record for the first time since 1992. Although their improved record boosted them all the way to second in the NL Central standings, the Brewers still failed to qualify for postseason play.

In 2008, Milwaukee's 26-year playoff drought finally came to an end. The team's core of Fielder, Braun, Hardy, and Suppan was helped by the signing of reliever Eric Gagne, a former Cy Young Award winner, and the acquisition of C. C. Sabathia, an ace pitcher who was obtained

A LEGENDARY LOGO

For the first seven years of their existence, the Milwaukee Brewers had an unremarkable logo that featured a "barrel man" swinging a bat. But in 1977, the team invited designers to submit drawings for a new logo and offered a prize of $2,000 to the winning artist. One of the more than 2,000 entries submitted was by Tom Meindel, a young student at the University of Wisconsin–Eau Claire. "I was a cash poor student, struggling to get by," Meindel says. "So I started sketching out ideas, but nothing seemed to work." Then Meindel tucked a lowercase *b* under a lowercase *m*. When he stepped back and looked at it, he realized that, together, the letters looked like a baseball glove. "Something rang true," Meindel realized. "It had a double meaning." Meindel's logo was selected by the team and used as its primary logo for 16 seasons. It was considered by many to be one of the most recognizable logos in professional sports, and fans were disappointed when it was replaced in 1994. In 2005, new team owner Mark Attanasio brought the logo, as well as the club's old pinstriped uniforms, back for "Retro Friday" home games.

Prince Fielder came by his slugging power naturally,
as he was the son of former Detroit Tigers star
Cecil Fielder, who clubbed 51 homers in 1990.

PRINCE FIELDER

in midseason via one of the biggest trades in franchise history. Sabathia had won the Cy Young Award in 2007 with Cleveland, and he pitched as if he wanted to win it again with Milwaukee. During the second half of the season, Sabathia posted an 11–2 record with an amazing 1.65 earned run average (ERA).

Brewers management was determined to make the most of its costly investments. So after the team lingered in second place throughout August and the first half of September, manager Ned Yost was fired and replaced by former bench coach Dale Sveum. The Brewers won 7 of their last 12 games under Sveum—not enough to ascend higher than second place but, with a 3–1 victory over the Chicago Cubs in the last game of the season, enough to send Milwaukee back to the playoffs as the Wild Card team. The Brewers' return was short-lived, however, as the Philadelphia Phillies topped them in the NL Division Series (NLDS) three games to one.

Sheets, Gagne, and Sabathia were all gone before the 2009 season started. However, 41-year-old closer Trevor Hoffman, the NL's all-time saves leader, joined the team and stepped up in a big way. Still, despite the impressive slugging

DAVE BUSH

quartet of Braun, Fielder, second baseman Rickie Weeks, and right fielder Corey Hart, the Brewers fell back below the .500 mark in both 2009 and 2010 before trading for ace pitcher Zack Greinke in late 2010.

Through thick and thin, the Brewers have built their history upon a simple approach—turning talented young players into longtime fan favorites. Those fans have supported their team from the home-run-happy days of the early 1980s through some forgettable seasons in the 1990s. Someday soon, they hope to throw ticker tape in the city's streets once again, this time for a world champion wearing Brewers blue and gold.

INDEX